MW01618432

Rabbi Nosson Scherman / Rabbi Gedaliah Zlotowitz
General Editors
Rabbi Meir Zlotowitz ז״ל, *Founder*

Sarah
Published by
ARTSCROLL®
Mesorah Publications, ltd

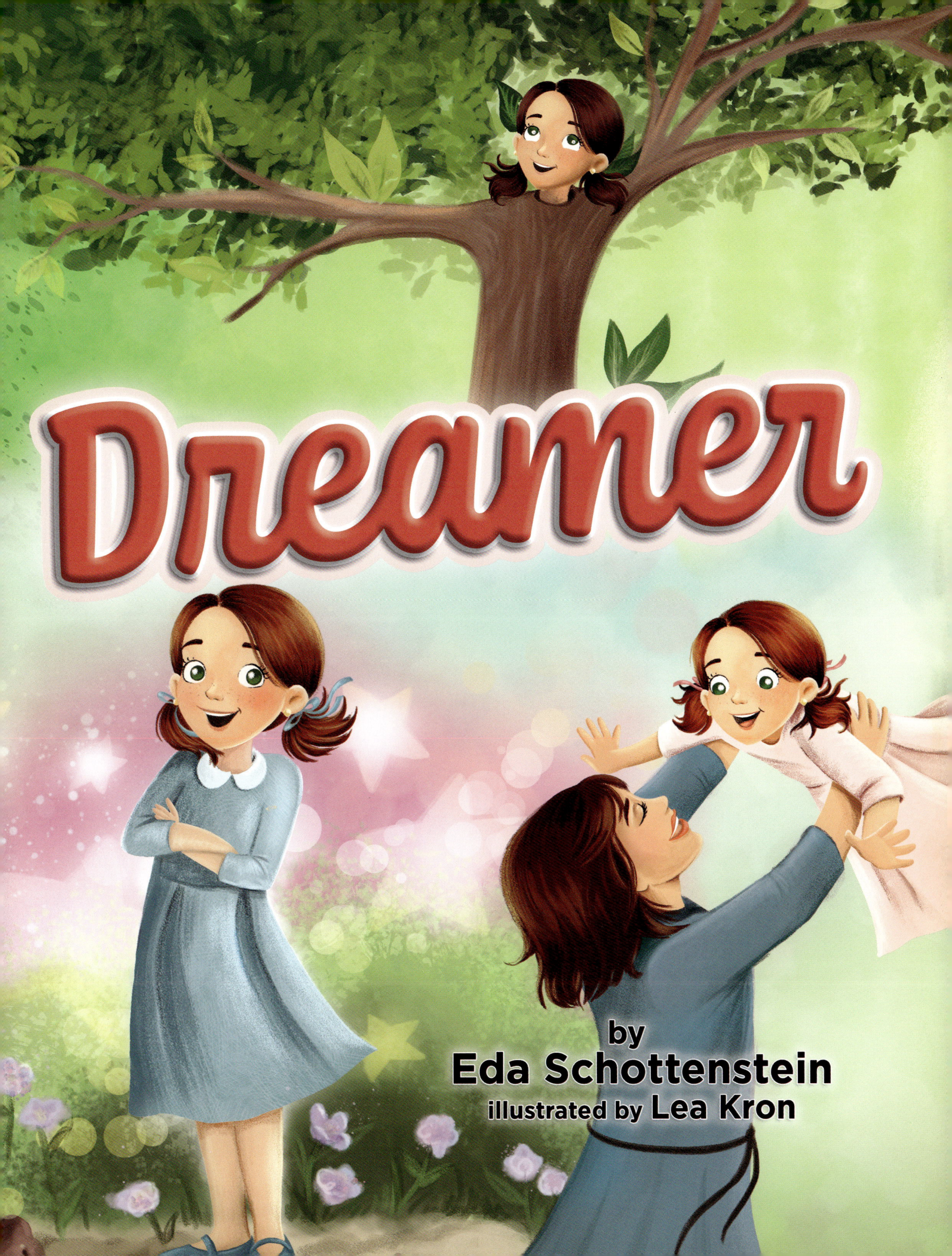
Dreamer
by
Eda Schottenstein
illustrated by Lea Kron

RTSCROLL® YOUTH SERIES

"SARAH DREAMER"

First impression: June 2020

Published by **MESORAH PUBLICATIONS, LTD.**
313 Regina Avenue / Rahway, N.J. 07065 / (718) 921-9000 / Fax: (718) 680-1875
www.artscroll.com

Illustrated by Lea Kron

Distributed in Israel by **SIFRIATI / A. GITLER**
POB 2351 / Bnei Brak 51122 / Israel

Distributed in Europe by **LEHMANNS**
Unit E, Viking Business Park, Rolling Mill Road / Jarrow, Tyne and Wear / England NE32 3DP

Distributed in Australia and New Zealand by **GOLDS WORLD OF JUDAICA**
3-13 William Street / Balaclava, Melbourne 3183, Victoria, Australia

Distributed in South Africa by **KOLLEL BOOKSHOP**
Northfield Centre / 17 Northfield Avenue / Glenhazel 2192 / Johannesburg, South Africa

Printed in PRC

ISBN-10: 1-4226-2592-3
ISBN-13: 978-1-4226-2592-7

Dedicated to

David, Ari,
Nina, Aliyah,
and Reeva

Little Sarah Dreamer
Saw a beautiful bird in the sky.
She watched with endless pleasure
And said, “I want to fly.

“Oh, how I wish I were a bird,
With big and colorful wings.”
“Sarah,” said her mother,
“You can be happy with your things.

"And when you're grateful for your strengths,
You won't need wings to fly.
Find your superpower, Sarah,
Soar in your own sky.

"And if sometimes you stumble,
Or feel you don't belong,
Don't give up, sweet Sarah,
Keep dreaming and stay strong.

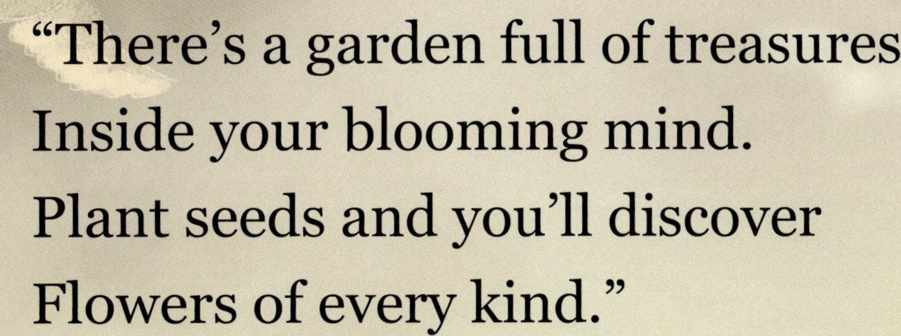

“There’s a garden full of treasures
Inside your blooming mind.
Plant seeds and you’ll discover
Flowers of every kind.”

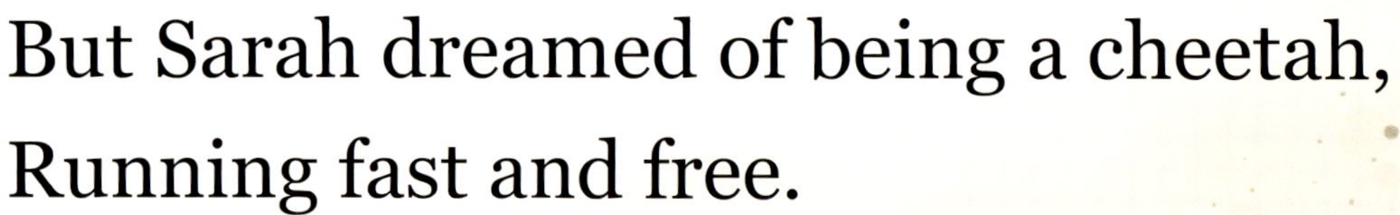

But Sarah dreamed of being a cheetah,
Running fast and free.
“Sarah,” said her mother,
“Tell me who *you* wish to be.

“There’s much that you can learn
From a cheetah’s lightning speed.
Run as quickly as you can,
To help a friend in need.

"Stay focused like a cheetah
When you feel like giving up.
Reach higher than you thought you could,
And know you're good enough."

The next day Sarah Dreamer
Saw a tall and wondrous tree.
She marveled at its beauty,
Its strength for all to see.

"I want to be just like that tree,
I want to be so tall."
"Sarah," whispered mommy,
"Though you might be small,

“You can stand tall when it counts,
Stand up for what is right.
Trees can teach to stay rooted
And still shine so bright.

“You might not understand this now,
But one day you will see
That you were meant to be created
Just as you should be.

"And when you see fast cheetahs,
Or admire the tallest tree,
I'll be there to remind you
How I love you endlessly.

“So be the friend you want to have,
Dance to your own drum.
Believe you will always be enough,
No matter where you’re from.

“Marvel at the birds you see,
Admire what they do.
But take a look inside yourself
To find your greatest you.

“Share your talents, use your gifts,
Don’t let them wither away.
Mistakes will happen, they often do,
Remember, that’s okay.

“On days when you feel grumpy
And don’t understand why,
Remember me, your biggest fan,
Let those feelings pass you by.

“Sleep tight, my dearest Sarah,
Tomorrow is another day,
To learn and laugh, to dream and love,
To dance and run and play.”

The next day Sarah Dreamer
Woke up and understood,
That she could change the way she thinks,
That she can make things good.

"Today I am Sarah Dreamer,
There's so much to be done.
I'll do the best I can today,
To make it great and fun.

“Oh Mommy, now I understand
That I might have been wrong.
But now I think I recognize
What you’ve known all along.

"I am Sarah Dreamer,
There's only one of me.
I'm strong, I'm brave, I'm wonderful,
Because I choose to be."